Reynolds Pamphlet

Reynolds Pamphlet

Alexander Hamilton

MINT EDITIONS

Reynolds Pamphlet was first published in 1797.

This edition published by Mint Editions 2021.

ISBN 9781513295619 | E-ISBN 9781513297118

Published by Mint Editions®

MINT EDITIONS

minteditionbooks.com

Publishing Director: Jennifer Newens
Design & Production: Rachel Lopez Metzger
Project Manager: Micaela Clark
Typesetting: Westchester Publishing Services

The spirit of jacobinism, if not entirely a new spirit, has at least been cloathed with a more gigantic body and armed with more powerful weapons than it ever before possessed. It is perhaps not too much to say, that it threatens more extensive and complicated mischiefs to the world than have hitherto flowed from the three great scourges of mankind, WAR, PESTILENCE and FAMINE. To what point it will ultimately lead society, it is impossible for human foresight to pronounce; but there is just ground to apprehend that its progress may be marked with calamities of which the dreadful incidents of the French revolution afford a very faint image. Incessantly busied in undermining all the props of public security and private happiness, it seems to threaten the political and moral world with a complete overthrow.

A principal engine, by which this spirit endeavours to accomplish its purposes is that of calumny. It is essential to its success that the influence of men of upright principles, disposed and able to resist its enterprises, shall be at all events destroyed. Not content with traducing their best efforts for the public good, with misrepresenting their purest motives, with inferring criminality from actions innocent or laudable, the most direct falshoods are invented and propagated, with undaunted effrontery and unrelenting perseverance. Lies often detected and refuted are still revived and repeated, in the hope that the refutation may have been forgotten or that the frequency and boldness of accusation may supply the place of truth and proof. The most profligate men are encouraged, probably bribed, certainly with patronage if not with money, to become informers and accusers. And when tales, which their characters alone ought to discredit, are refuted by evidence and facts which oblige the patrons of them to abandon their support, they still continue in corroding whispers to wear away the reputations which they could not directly subvert. If, luckily for the conspirators against honest fame, any little foible or folly can be traced out in one, whom they desire to persecute, it becomes at once in their hands a two-edged sword, by which to wound the public character and stab the private felicity of the person. With such men, nothing is sacred. Even the peace of an unoffending and amiable wife is a welcome repast to their insatiate fury against the husband.

In the gratification of this baleful spirit, we not only hear the jacobin news-papers continually ring with odious insinuations and charges against many of our most virtuous citizens; but, not satisfied with this, a measure new in this country has been lately adopted to give greater efficacy to the system of defamation—periodical pamphlets issue from the same presses, full freighted with misrepresentation and falshood, artfully calculated to hold up the opponents of the FACTION to the jealousy and distrust of the present generation and if possible, to transmit their names with dishonor to posterity. Even the great and multiplied services, the tried and rarely equalled virtues of a WASHINGTON, can secure no exemption.

How then can I, with pretensions every way inferior expect to escape? And if truly this be, as every appearance indicates, a conspiracy of vice against virtue, ought I not rather to be flattered, that I have been so long and so peculiarly an object of persecution? Ought I to regret, if there be any thing about me, so formidable to the Faction as to have made me worthy to be distinguished by the plentytude of its rancour and venom?

It is certain that I have had a pretty copious experience of its malignity. For the honor of human nature, it is to be hoped that the examples are not numerous of men so greatly calumniated and persecuted, as I have been, with so little cause.

I dare appeal to my immediate fellow citizens of whatever political party for the truth of the assertion, that no man ever carried into public life a more unblemished pecuniary reputation, than that with which I undertook the office of Secretary of the Treasury; a character marked by an indifference to the acquisition of property rather than an avidity for it.

With such a character, however natural it was to expect criticism and opposition, as to the political principles which I might manifest or be supposed to entertain, as to the wisdom or expediency of the plans, which I might propose, or as to the skill, care or diligence with which the business of my department might be executed, it was not natural to expect nor did I expect that my fidelity or integrity in a pecuniary sense would ever be called in question.

But on his head a mortifying disappointment has been experienced. Without the slightest foundation, I have been repeatedly held up to the suspicions of the world as a man directed in his administration by the most sordid views; who did not scruple to sacrifice the public to his private interest, his duty and honor to the sinister accumulation of wealth.

Merely because I *retained* an opinion once common to me and the most influencial of those who opposed me, *That the public debt ought to be provided for on the basis of the contract upon which it was created*, I have been wickedly accused with wantonly increasing the public burthen many millions, in order to promote a stockjobbing interest of myself and friends.

Merely because a member of the House of Representatives entertained a different idea from me, as to the legal effect of appropriation laws, and did not understand accounts, I was exposed to the imputation of having committed a deliberate and criminal violation of the laws and to the suspicion of being a defaulter for millions; so as to have been driven to the painful necessity of calling for a formal and solemn inquiry.

The inquiry took place. It was conducted by a committee of fifteen members of the House of Representatives—a majority of them either my decided political enemies or inclined against me, some of them the most active and intelligent of my opponents, without a single man, who being known to be friendly to me, possessed also such knowledge and experience of public affairs as would enable him to counteract injurious intrigues. Mr. Giles of Virginia who had commenced the attack was of the committee.[1]

The officers and books of the treasury were examined. The transactions between the several banks and the treasury were scrutinized. Even my *private accounts* with those institutions were laid open to the committee; and every possible facility given to the inquiry. The result was a complete demonstration that the suspicions which had been entertained were groundless.

Those which had taken the fastest hold were, that the public monies had been made subservient to loans, discounts and accommodations to myself and friends. The committee in reference to this point reported thus: "It appears from the affidavits of the Cashier and several officers of the bank of the United States and several of the directors, the Cashier, and other officers of the bank of NewYork, that the Secretary of the Treasury never has either *directly* or *indirectly*, for himself or any other person, procured any discount or credit from either of the said banks upon the basis of any public monies which at any time have been deposited therein under his direction: And the committee are *satisfied*, that *no monies* of the United States, whether *before* or *after* they have

---

1. This investigation into H's conduct as Secretary of the Treasury took place from December, 1793, to May, 1794. For this investigation and William B. Giles's role in it, see the introductory note to H to Frederick A. C. Muhlenberg, December 16, 1793.

passed to the credit of the Treasurer have ever been *directly* or *indirectly* used for or applied to *any purposes* but those of the government, except so far as all monies deposited in a bank are concerned in the *general operations* thereof."[2]

The report, which I have always understood was unanimous, contains in other respects, with considerable detail the materials of a complete exculpation. My enemies, finding no handle for their malice, abandoned the pursuit.

Yet unwilling to leave any ambiguity upon the point, when I determined to resign my office, I gave early previous notice of it to the House of Representatives, for the declared purpose of affording an opportunity for legislative crimination, if any ground for it had been discovered.[3] Not the least step towards it was taken. From which I have a right to infer the universal conviction of the House, that no cause existed, and to consider the result as a complete vindication.

On another occasion, a worthless man of the name of Fraunces found encouragement to bring forward to the House of Representatives a formal charge against me of unfaithful conduct in office.[4] A Committee of the House was appointed to inquire, consisting in this case also, partly of some of my most intelligent and active enemies. The issue was an unanimous exculpation of me as will appear by the following extract from the Journals of the House of Representatives of the 19th of February 1794.

"The House resumed the consideration of the report of the Committee, to whom was referred the memorial of Andrew G. Fraunces: whereupon,

"*Resolved*, That the reasons assigned by the secretary of the treasury, for refusing payment of the warrants referred to in the memorial, are fully sufficient to justify his conduct; and that in the whole course of this transaction, the secretary and other officers of the treasury, have acted a meritorious part towards the public."

"*Resolved*, That the charge exhibited in the memorial, against the secretary of the treasury, relative to the purchase of the pension of Baron de Glaubeck is wholly illiberal and groundless."[5]

---

2. H is quoting from the report of the select committee appointed to investigate H's conduct as Secretary of the Treasury, May 22, 1794 (D, RG 233, Papers of the Select Committee Appointed to Examine the Treasury Department, Third Congress, National Archives).

3. See H to Frederick A. C. Muhlenberg, December 1, 1794.

4. See the introductory note to Andrew G. Fraunces to H, May 16, 1793.

5. *Journal of the House*, II, 67.

Was it not to have been expected that these repeated demonstrations of the injustice of the accusations hazarded against me would have abashed the enterprise of my calumniators? However natural such an expectation may seem, it would betray an ignorance of the true character of the Jacobin system. It is a maxim deeply ingrafted in that dark system, that no character, however upright, is a match for constantly reiterated attacks, however false. It is well understood by its disciples, that every calumny makes some proselites and even retains some; since justification seldom circulates as rapidly and as widely as slander. The number of those who from doubt proceed to suspicion and thence to belief of imputed guilt is continually augmenting; and the public mind fatigued at length with resistance to the calumnies which eternally assail it, is apt in the end to sit down with the opinion that a person so often accused cannot be entirely innocent.

Relying upon this weakness of human nature, the Jacobin Scandal-Club though often defeated constantly return to the charge. Old calumnies are served up a-fresh and every pretext is seized to add to the catalogue. The person whom they seek to blacken, by dint of repeated strokes of their brush, becomes a demon in their own eyes, though he might be pure and bright as an angel but for the daubing of those wizard painters.

Of all the vile attempts which have been made to injure my character that which has been lately revived in No. V and VI, of the history of the United States for 1796 is the most vile.[6] This it will be impossible for any *intelligent*, I will not say *candid*, man to doubt, when he shall have accompanied me through the examination.

I owe perhaps to my friends an apology for condescending to give a public explanation. A just pride with reluctance stoops to a formal vindication against so despicable a contrivance and is inclined rather to oppose to it the uniform evidence of an upright character. This would be my conduct on the present occasion, did not the tale seem to derive a sanction from the names of three men[7] of some weight and consequence in the society: a circumstance, which I trust will excuse me

---

6. James Thomson Callender, The History of the United States for 1796; Including a Variety of Interesting Particulars Relative to the Federal Government Previous to that Period (Philadelphia: Snowden & McCorkle, 1797). For information on the publication of this pamphlet, see Wolcott to H, July 3, 1797, note 1.

7. James Monroe, Frederick A. C. Muhlenberg, and Abraham B. Venable.

for paying attention to a slander that without this prop, would defeat itself by intrinsic circumstances of absurdity and malice.

The charge against me is a connection with one James Reynolds for purposes of improper pecuniary speculation. My real crime is an amorous connection with his wife, for a considerable time with his privity and connivance, if not originally brought on by a combination between the husband and wife with the design to extort money from me.

This confession is not made without a blush. I cannot be the apologist of any vice because the ardour of passion may have made it mine. I can never cease to condemn myself for the pang, which it may inflict in a bosom eminently intitled to all my gratitude, fidelity and love. But that bosom will approve, that even at so great an expence, I should effectually wipe away a more serious stain from a name, which it cherishes with no less elevation than tenderness. The public too will I trust excuse the confession. The necessity of it to my defence against a more heinous charge could alone have extorted from me so painful an indecorum.

Before I proceed to an exhibition of the positive proof which repels the charge, I shall analize the documents from which it is deduced, and I am mistaken if with discerning and candid minds more would be necessary. But I desire to obviate the suspicions of the most suspicious.

The first reflection which occurs on a perusal of the documents is that it is morally impossible I should have been foolish as well as depraved enough to employ so vile an instrument as *Reynolds* for such *insignificant ends*, as are indicated by different parts of the story itself. My enemies to be sure have kindly pourtrayed me as another *Chartres*[8] on the score of moral principle. But they have been ever bountiful in ascribing to me talents. It has suited their purpose to exaggerate such as I may possess, and to attribute to them an influence to which they are not intitled. But the present accusation imputes to me as much folly as wickedness. All the documents shew, and it is otherwise matter of notoriety, that Reynolds was an obscure, unimportant and profligate man. Nothing could be more weak, because nothing could be more

---

8. In 1793 Louis Philippe d'Orleans, duc de Chartres, the son of Louis Philippe Joseph, duc d'Orleans, deserted to the Austrians with his commander, General Charles François Dumouriez. Louis Philippe spent three years in exile in northern Europe. In 1796 the Directory agreed to release from prison his two brothers, the Duc de Montpensier and the Duc de Beaujolais, if Louis Philippe would go to America. The Duc de Chartres arrived in Philadelphia in October, 1796, and his brothers joined him there in February, 1797. Louis Philippe was King of France from 1830 to 1848.

ALEXANDER HAMILTON

unsafe than to make use of such an instrument; to use him too without any intermediate agent more worthy of confidence who might keep me out of sight, to write him numerous letters recording the objects of the improper connection (for this is pretended and that the letters were afterwards burnt at my request) to unbosom myself to him with a prodigality of confidence, by very unnecessarily telling him, as he alleges, of a connection in speculation between myself and Mr. Duer.[9] It is very extraordinary, if the head of the money department of a country, being unprincipled enough to sacrifice his trust and his integrity, could not have contrived objects of profit sufficiently large to have engaged the co-operation of men of far greater importance than Reynolds, and with whom there could have been due safety, and should have been driven to the necessity of unkennelling such a reptile to be the instrument of his cupidity.

But, moreover, the scale of the concern with Reynolds, such as it is presented, is contemptibly narrow for a rapacious speculating secretary of the treasury. *Clingman, Reynolds* and his wife were manifestly in very close confidence with each other. It seems there was a free communication of secrets. Yet in clubbing their different items of information as to the supplies of money which Reynolds received from me, what do they amount to? *Clingman* states, that Mrs. Reynolds told him, that at a certain time her husband had received from me upwards of eleven hundred dollars.[10] A note is produced which shews that at one time fifty dollars were sent to him,[11] and another note is produced, by which and the information of Reynolds himself through Clingman, it appears that at another time 300 dollars were asked[12] and refused. Another sum of 200 dollars is spoken of by *Clingman* as having been furnished to Reynolds at some other time.[13] What a scale of speculation is this for the head of a public treasury, for one who in the very publication that brings forward the charge is represented as having procured to be funded at forty millions a debt which ought to have been discharged at

9. William Duer.
10. Clingman's deposition, dated December 13, 1792, is document No. IV (a) in the appendix to this pamphlet.
11. James Reynolds to H, June 23, 1792, which is document No. XX in the appendix to this pamphlet.
12. James Reynolds to H, June 3–22, 1792, which is document No. XIX in the appendix to this pamphlet.
13. Clingman's deposition, dated December 13, 1792, is document No. IV (a) in the appendix to this pamphlet.

ten or fifteen millions for the criminal purpose of enriching himself and his friends? He must have been a clumsy knave, if he did not secure enough of this excess of twenty five or thirty millions, to have taken away all inducement to risk his character in such bad hands and in so huckstering a way—or to have enabled him, if he did employ such an agent, to do it with more means and to better purpose. It is curious, that this rapacious secretary should at one time have furnished his speculating agent with the paltry sum of fifty dollars, at another, have refused him the inconsiderable sum of 300 dollars, declaring upon his honor that it was not in his power to furnish it. This declaration was true or not; if the last the refusal ill comports with the idea of a speculating connection—if the first, it is very singular that the head of the treasury engaged without scruple in schemes of profit should have been destitute of so small a sum. But if we suppose this officer to be living upon an inadequate salary, without any collateral pursuits of gain, the appearances then are simple and intelligible enough, applying to them the true key.

It appears that *Reynolds* and *Clingman* were detected by the then comptroller of the treasury,[14] in the odious crime of suborning a witness to commit perjury, for the purpose of obtaining letters of administration on the estate of a person who was living in order to receive a small sum of money due to him from the treasury.[15] It is certainly extraordinary that the confidential agent of the head of that department should have been in circumstances to induce a resort to so miserable an expedient. It is odd, if there was a speculating connection, that it was not more profitable both to the secretary and to his agent than are indicated by the circumstances disclosed.

It is also a remarkable and very instructive fact, that notwithstanding the great confidence and intimacy, which subsisted between *Clingman,* *Reynolds* and his wife, and which continued till after the period of the liberation of the two former from the prosecution against them, neither of them has ever specified the objects of the pretended connection in speculation between Reynolds and me. The pretext that the letters which contained the evidence were destroyed is no answer. They could not have been forgotten and might have been disclosed from memory. The total omission of this could only have proceeded from the

---

14. Oliver Wolcott, Jr.

15. The perjurer was John Delabar. The claimant was Ephraim Goodenough. See Wolcott to H, July 3, 1797, note 14.

ALEXANDER HAMILTON

consideration that detail might have led to detection. The destruction of letters besides is a fiction, which is refuted not only by the general improbability, that I should put myself upon paper with so despicable a person on a subject which might expose me to infamy, but by the evidence of extreme caution on my part in this particular, resulting from the laconic and disguised form of the notes which are produced. They prove incontestibly that there was an unwillingness to trust Reynolds with my hand writing. The true reason was, that I apprehended he might make use of it to impress upon others the belief of some pecuniary connection with me, and besides implicating my character might render it the engine of a false credit, or turn it to some other sinister use. Hence the disguise; for my conduct in admitting at once and without hesitation that the notes were from me proves that it was never my intention by the expedient of disguising my hand to shelter myself from any serious inquiry.

The accusation against me was never heard of 'till Clingman and Reynolds were under prosecution by the treasury for an infamous crime. It will be seen by the document No. 1 (a) that during the endeavours of *Clingman* to obtain relief, through the interposition of Mr. Mughlenberg, he made to the latter the communication of my pretended criminality. It will be further seen by document No. 2 ([a]) that Reynolds had while in prison conveyed to the ears of Messrs. Monroe and Venable that he could give intelligence of my being concerned in speculation, and that he also supposed that he was kept in prison by a design on my part to oppress him and drive him away. And by his letter to *Clingman* of the 13 of December, after he was released from prison, it also appears that he was actuated by a spirit of revenge against me; for he declares that he will have *satisfaction* from me *at all events;* adding, as addressed to *Clingman*, "And *you only I trust*."[16]

Three important inferences flow from these circumstances—one that the accusation against me was an auxiliary to the efforts of *Clingman* and *Reynolds* to get released from a disgraceful prosecution—another that there was a vindicative spirit against me at least on the part of Reynolds—the third, that he confided in *Clingman* as a coadjutor in the plan of vengeance. These circumstances, according to every estimate of the credit due to accusers, ought to destroy their testimony. To what credit are persons intitled, who in telling a story are governed by the

---

16. See H to James Monroe, July 20, 1797, note 4.

double motive of escaping from disgrace and punishment and of gratifying revenge? As to Mrs. Reynolds, if she was not an accomplice, as it is too probable she was, her situation would naturally subject her to the will of her husband. But enough besides will appear in the sequel to shew that her testimony merits no attention.

The letter which has been just cited deserves a more particular attention. As it was produced by Clingman, there is a chasm of three lines, which lines are manifestly essential to explain the sense. It may be inferred from the context, that these deficient lines would unfold the cause of the resentment which is expressed. 'Twas from them that might have been learnt the true nature of the transaction. The expunging of them is a violent presumption that they would have contradicted the purpose for which the letter was produced. A witness offering such a mutilated piece descredits himself. The mutilation is alone satisfactory proof of contrivance and imposition. The manner of accounting for it is frivolous.

The words of the letter are strong—satisfaction is to be had *at all events, per fas et nefas*, and *Clingman* is the chosen confidential agent of the laudable plan of vengeance. It must be confessed he was not wanting in his part.

Reynolds, as will be seen by No. II (a) alleges that a merchant came to him and offered as a volunteer to be his bail, who he suspected had been instigated to it by me, and after being decoyed to the place the merchant wished to carry him to, he refused being his bail, unless he would deposit a sum of money to some considerable amount which he could not do and was in consequence committed to prison. Clingman (No. IV a) tells the same story in substance though with some difference in form leaving to be implied what Reynolds expresses and naming *Henry Seckel* as the merchant. The deposition of this respectable citizen (No. XXIII) gives the lie to both, and shews that he was in fact the agent of *Clingman*, from motives of good will to him, as his former book-keeper, that he never had any communication with me concerning either of them till after they were both in custody, that when he came as a messenger to me from one of them, I not only declined interposing in their behalf, but informed Mr. Seckel that they had been guilty of a crime and advised him to have nothing to do with them.

This single fact goes far to invalidate the whole story. It shews p(l)ainly the disregard of truth and the malice by which the parties were actuated. Other important inferences are to be drawn from the transaction. Had I been conscious that I had any thing to fear from *Reynolds* of the nature which has been pretended, should I have warned Mr. *Seckel* against having any thing to do with them? Should I not rather have encouraged him to have come to their assistance? Should I not have been eager to promote their liberation? But this is not the only instance, in which I acted a contrary part. *Clingman* testifies in No. V that I would not permit *Fraunces* a clerk in my office to become their bail, but signified to him that if he did it, he must quit the department.[17]

Clingman states in No. IV (a) that my note in answer to Reynolds' application for a loan towards a subscription to the *Lancaster Turnpike* was in his possession from about the time it was written (June 1792.) This circumstance, apparently trivial, is very explanatory. To what end had *Clingman* the custody of this note all that time if it was not part of a project to lay the foundation for some false accusation?

It appears from No. V[18] that *Fraunces* had said, or was stated to have said, something to my prejudice. If my memory serves me aright, it was that he had been my agent in some speculations. When *Fraunces* was interrogated concerning it, he absolutely denied that he had said any thing of the kind. The charge which this same *Fraunces* afterwards preferred against me to the House of Representatives, and the fate of it, have been already mentioned. It is illustrative of the nature of the combination which was formed against me.

There are other features in the documents which are relied upon to constitute the charge against me, that are of a nature to corroborate the inference to be drawn from the particulars which have been noticed. But there is no need to be over minute. I am much mistaken if the view which has been taken of the subject is not sufficient, without any thing further, to establish my innocence with every discerning and fair mind.

I proceed in the next place to offer a frank and plain solution of the enigma, by giving a history of the origin and progress of my connection with Mrs. Reynolds, of its discovery, real and pretended by the husband, and of the disagreeable embarrassments to which it exposed me. This history will be supported by the letters of Mr. and Mrs. Reynolds, which leave no room for doubt of the principal facts, and at the same

---

17. H mistakenly referred to document "No. V." He is actually referring to document No. IV (a) in the appendix to this pamphlet.

18. H is referring to document No. V in James Thomson Callender's *History.* See Wolcott to H, July 3, 1797, notes 1, 50, and 51.

time explain with precision the objects of the little notes from me which have been published, shewing clearly that such of them as have related to money had no reference to any concern in speculation. As the situation which will be disclosed, will fully explain every ambiguous appearance, and meet satisfactorily the written documents, nothing more can be requisite to my justification. For frail indeed will be the tenure by which the most blameless man will hold his reputation, if the assertions of three of the most abandoned characters in the community, two of them stigmatized by the discrediting crime which has been mentioned, are sufficient to blast it. The business of accusation would soon become in such a case, a regular trade, and men's reputations would be bought and sold like any marketable commodity.

Some time in the summer of the year 1791 a woman called at my house in the city of Philadelphia[19] and asked to speak with me in private. I attended her into a room apart from the family. With a seeming air of affliction she informed that she was a daughter of a Mr. Lewis, sister to a Mr. G. Livingston of the State of New-York, and wife to a Mr. Reynolds whose father was in the Commissary Department during the war with Great Britain, that her husband, who for a long time had treated her very cruelly, had lately left her, to live with another woman, and in so destitute a condition, that though desirous of returning to her friends she had not the means—that knowing I was a citizen of New-York, she had taken the liberty to apply to my humanity for assistance.

I replied, that her situation was a very interesting one—that I was disposed to afford her assistance to convey her to her friends, but this at the moment not being convenient to me (which was the fact) I must request the place of her residence, to which I should bring or send a small supply of money. She told me the street and the number of the house where she lodged. In the evening I put a bank-bill in my pocket and went to the house.[20] I inquired for Mrs. Reynolds and was shewn up stairs, at the head of which she met me and conducted me into a bed room. I took the bill out of my pocket and gave it to her. Some conversation ensued from which it was quickly apparent that other than pecuniary consolation would be acceptable.

---

19. 79 South Third Street.

20. A Philadelphia directory for 1791 states that a "Mrs. Reynolds" lived at 154 South Fourth Street (Clement Biddle, *The Philadelphia Directory* (Philadelphia: Printed by James & Johnson, No. 147, High-Street, 1791), 107).

After this, I had frequent meetings with her, most of them at my own house; Mrs. Hamilton with her children being absent on a visit to her father.[21] In the course of a short time, she mentioned to me that her husband had solicited a reconciliation, and affected to consult me about it. I advised to it, and was soon after informed by her that it had taken place. She told me besides that her husband had been engaged in speculation, and she believed could give information respecting the conduct of some persons in the department which would be useful. I sent for Reynolds who came to me accordingly.

In the course of our interview, he confessed that he had obtained a list of claims from a person in my department which he had made use of in his speculations. I invited him, by the expectation of my friendship and good offices, to disclose the person. After some affectation of scruple, he pretended to yield, and ascribed the infidelity to Mr. Duer from whom he said he had obtained the list in New-York, while he (Duer) was in the department.

As Mr. Duer had resigned his office some time before the seat of government was removed to Philadelphia; this discovery, if it had been true, was not very important—yet it was the interest of my passions to appear to set value upon it, and to continue the expectation of friendship and good offices. Mr. Reynolds told me he was going to Virginia, and on his return would point out something in which I could serve him. I do not know but he said something about employment in a public office.

On his return he asked employment as a clerk in the treasury department. The knowledge I had acquired of him was decisive against such a request. I parried it by telling him, what was true, that there was no vacancy in my immediate office, and that the appointment of clerks in the other branches of the department was left to the chiefs of the respective branches. Reynolds alleged, as *Clingman* relates No. IV (a) as a topic of complaint against me that I had promised him *employment* and had *disappointed* him. The situation with the wife would naturally incline me to conciliate this man. It is possible I may have used vague expressions which raised expectation; but the more I learned of the person, the more inadmissible his employment in a public office became. Some material reflections will occur here to a discerning mind. Could I

---

21. Elizabeth Hamilton left Philadelphia for a visit with her parents in Albany in the middle of July, 1791. See H to Rufus King, July 8, 1791; H to Elizabeth Hamilton, July 27, 1791.

have preferred my private gratification to the public interest, should I not have found the employment he desired for a man, whom it was so convenient to me, on my own statement, to lay under obligations. Had I had any such connection with him, as he has since pretended, is it likely that he would have wanted other employment? Or is it likely that wanting it, I should have hazarded his resentment by a persevering refusal? This little circumstance shews at once the delicacy of my conduct, in its public relations, and the impossibility of my having had the connection pretended with Reynolds.

The intercourse with Mrs. Reynolds, in the mean time, continued; and, though various reflections, (in which a further knowledge of Reynolds' character and the suspicion of some concert between the husband and wife bore a part) induced me to wish a cessation of it; yet her conduct, made it extremely difficult to disentangle myself. All the appearances of violent attachment, and of agonizing distress at the idea of a relinquishment, were played off with a most imposing art. This, though it did not make me entirely the dupe of the plot, yet kept me in a state of irresolution. My sensibility, perhaps my vanity, admitted the possibility of a real fondness; and led me to adopt the plan of a gradual discontinuance rather than of a sudden interruption, as least calculated to give pain, if a real partiality existed.

Mrs. Reynolds, on the other hand, employed every effort to keep up my attention and visits. Her pen was freely employed, and her letters were filled with those tender and pathetic effusions which would have been natural to a woman truly fond and neglected.

One day, I received a letter from her, which is in the appendix (No. I. b) intimating a discovery by her husband. It was matter of doubt with me whether there had been really a discovery by accident, or whether the time for the catastrophe of the plot was arrived.

The same day, being the 15th of December 1791, I received from Mr. Reynolds the letter (No. II. b) by which he informs me of the detection of his wife in the act of writing a letter to me, and that he had obtained from her a discovery of her connection with me, suggesting that it was the consequence of an undue advantage taken of her distress.

In answer to this I sent him a note, or message desiring him to call upon me at my office, which I think he did the same day.[22]

---

22. Letter not found.

He in substance repeated the topics contained in his letter, and concluded as he had done there, that he was resolved to have satisfaction.

I replied that he knew best what evidence he had of the alleged connection between me and his wife, that I neither admitted nor denied it—that if he knew of any injury I had done him, intitling him to satisfaction, it lay with him to name it.

He travelled over the same ground as before, and again concluded with the same vague claim of satisfaction, but without specifying the kind, which would content him. It was easy to understand that he wanted money, and to prevent an explosion, I resolved to gratify him. But willing to manage his delicacy, if he had any, I reminded him that I had at our first interview made him a promise of service, that I was disposed to do it as far as might be proper, and in my power, and requested him to consider in what manner I could do it, and to write to me. He withdrew with a promise of compliance.

Two days after, the 17th of December, he wrote me the letter (No. III. b). The evident drift of this letter is to exaggerate the injury done by me, to make a display of sensibility and to magnify the atonement, which was to be required. It however comes to no conclusion, but proposes a meeting at the *George Tavern*, or at some other place more agreeable to me, which I should name.

On receipt of this letter, I called upon Reynolds, and assuming a decisive tone, told him, that I was tired of his indecision, and insisted upon his declaring to me explicitly what it was he aimed at. He again promised to explain by letter.

On the 19th, I received the promised letter (No. IV. b) the essence of which is that he was willing to take a thousand dollars as the plaister of his wounded honor.

I determined to give it to him, and did so in two payments, as per receipts (No. V and VI) dated the 22d of December and 3d of January. It is a little remarkable, that an avaricious speculating secretary of the treasury should have been so straitened for money as to be obliged to satisfy an engagement of this sort by two different payments!

On the 17th of January, I received the letter No. V[23] by which Reynolds invites me to *renew my visits to his wife*. He had before requested that I would see her no more. The motive to this step appears

---

23. H is mistaken, for he intended to refer to document No. VII in the appendix to this pamphlet.

in the conclusion of the letter, "*I rely* upon your befriending me, *if there should any thing offer that should be to my advantage*, as you *express a wish to befriend me*." Is the pre-existence of a speculating connection reconcileable with this mode of expression?

If I recollect rightly, I did not immediately accept the invitation, nor 'till after I had received several very importunate letters from Mrs. Reynolds—See her letters No. VIII, (b) IX, X.

On the 24th of March following, I received a letter from *Reynolds*, No. XI, and on the same day one from his wife, No. XII. These letters will further illustrate the obliging co-operation of the husband with his wife to aliment and keep alive my connection with her.

The letters from Reynolds, No. XIII to XVI, are an additional comment upon the same plan. It was a persevering scheme to spare no pains to levy contributions upon my passions on the one hand, and upon my apprehensions of discovery on the other. It is probably to No. XIV that my note, in these words, was an answer; "Tomorrow what is requested will be done. 'Twill hardly be possible *today*."[24] The letter presses for the loan which is asked for *today*. A scarcity of cash, which was not very uncommon, is believed to have modelled the reply.

The letter No. XVII is a master-piece. The husband there forbids my future visits to his wife, chiefly because I was careful to avoid publicity. It was probably necessary to the project of some deeper treason against me that I should be seen at the house. Hence was it contrived, with all the caution on my part to avoid it, that *Clingman* should occasionally see me.

The interdiction was every way welcome, and was I believe, strictly observed. On the second of June following, I received the letter No. XVIII, from Mrs. Reynolds, which proves that it was not her plan yet to let me off. It was probably the prelude to the letter from Reynolds, No. XIX, soliciting a *loan* of 300 dollars towards a subscription to the Lancaster Turnpike. *Clingman's* statement, No. IV ([a]), admits, on the information of Reynolds, that to this letter the following note from me was an answer—"*It is utterly out of my power I assure you 'pon my honour to comply with your request. Your note is returned*." The letter itself demonstrates, that here was no concern in speculation on my part— that the money is asked as a *favour* and as a *loan*, to be reimbursed

---

24. H to James Reynolds, April 7, 1792.

simply and without profit *in less than a fortnight*. My answer shews that even the loan was refused.

The letter No. XX, from *Reynolds*, explains the object of my note in these words, "*Inclosed are* 50 *dollars, they could not be sent sooner*,"[25] proving that this sum also was begged for in a very apologetic stile as a mere loan.

The letters of the 24th and 30th of August, No. XXI and XXII, furnish the key to the affair of the 200 dollars mentioned by *Clingman* in No. IV, shewing that this sum likewise was asked by way of loan, towards furnishing a small boarding-house which *Reynolds* and his wife were or pretended to be about to set up.

These letters collectively, furnish a complete elucidation of the nature of my transactions with *Reynolds*. They resolve them into an amorous connection with his wife, detected, or pretended to be detected by the husband, imposing on me the necessity of a pecuniary composition with him, and leaving me afterwards under a duress for fear of disclosure, which was the instrument of levying upon me from time to time *forced loans*. They apply directly to this state of things, the notes which *Reynolds* was so careful to preserve, and which had been employed to excite suspicion.

Four, and the principal of these notes have been not only generally, but particularly explained—I shall briefly notice the remaining two.

"My dear Sir, I expected to have heard the day after I had the pleasure of seeing you." This fragment, if truly part of a letter to *Reynolds*, denotes nothing more than a disposition to be civil to a man, whom, as I said before, it was the interest of my passions to conciliate. But I verily believe it was not part of a letter to him, because I do not believe that I ever addressed him in such a stile. It may very well have been part of a letter to some other person, procured by means of which I am ignorant, or it may have been the beginning of an intended letter, torn off, thrown into the chimney in my office, which was a common practice, and there or after it had been swept out picked up by Reynolds or some coadjutor of his. There appears to have been more than one clerk in the department some how connected with him.

The endeavour shewn by the letter No. XVII, to induce me to render my visits to Mrs. Reynolds more public, and the great care with which my little notes were preserved, justify the belief that at a period, before

---

25. H to James Reynolds, June 24, 1792.

it was attempted, the idea of implicating me in some accusation, with a view to the advantage of the accusers, was entertained. Hence the motive to pick up and preserve any fragment which might favour the idea of friendly or confidential correspondence.

2dly. "The person Mr. Reynolds inquired for on Friday waited for him all the evening at his house from a little after seven. Mr. R. may see him at any time today or tomorrow between the hours of two and three."

Mrs. Reynolds more than once communicated to me, that Reynolds would occasionally relapse into discontent to his situation—would treat her very ill—hint at the assassination of me—and more openly threaten, by way of revenge, to inform Mrs. Hamilton—all this naturally gave some uneasiness. I could not be absolutely certain whether it was artifice or reality. In the workings of human inconsistency, it was very possible, that the same man might be corrupt enough to compound for his wife's chastity and yet have sensibility enough to be restless in the situation and to hate the cause of it.

Reflections like these induced me for some time to use palliatives with the ill humours which were announced to me. Reynolds had called upon me in one of these discontented moods real or pretended. I was unwilling to provoke him by the appearance of neglect—and having failed to be at home at the hour he had been permitted to call, I wrote her the above note to obviate an ill impression.

The foregoing narrative and the remarks accompanying it have prepared the way for a perusal of the letters themselves. The more attention is used in this, the more entire will be the satisfaction which they will afford.

It has been seen that an explanation on the subject was had cotemporarily that is in December 1792, with three members of Congress—F. A. Muhlenberg, J. Monroe, and A. Venable. It is proper that the circumstances of this transaction should be accurately understood.

The manner in which Mr. Muhlenberg became engaged in the affair is fully set forth in the document (No. I. a). It is not equally clear how the two other gentlemen came to embark in it. The phraseology, in reference to this point in the close of (No. I. ([a])) and beginning of (No. II. ([a])) is rather equivocal. The gentlemen, if they please, can explain it.

But on the morning of the 15th of December 1792, the above mentioned gentlemen presented themselves at my office. Mr. Muhlenberg was then speaker. He introduced the subject by observing to me, that they *had discovered a very improper connection* between me and a Mr. Reynolds: extremely hurt by this mode of introduction, I arrested the progress of the discourse by giving way to very strong expressions of indignation. The gentlemen explained, telling me in substance that I had misapprehended them—that they did not intend to take the fact for established—that their meaning was to apprise me that unsought by them, information had been given them of an improper pecuniary connection between Mr. Reynolds and myself; that they had thought it their duty to pursue it and had become possessed of some documents of a suspicious complexion—that they had contemplated the laying the matter before the President, but before they did this, they thought it right to apprise me of the affair and to afford an opportunity of explanation; declaring at the same time that their agency in the matter was influenced solely by a sense of public duty and by no motive of personal ill will. If my memory be correct, the notes from me in a disguised hand were now shewn to me which without a moment's hesitation I acknowledged to be mine.

I replied, that the affair was now put upon a different footing—that I always stood ready to meet fair inquiry with frank communication—that it happened, in the present instance, to be in my power by written documents to remove all doubt as to the real nature of the business, and fully to convince, that nothing of the kind imputed to me did in fact exist. The same evening at my house was by mutual consent appointed for an explanation.

I immediately after saw Mr. Wolcott, and for the first time informed him of the affair and of the interview just had; and delivering into his hands for perusal the documents of which I was possessed, I engaged him to be present at the intended explanation in the evening.

In the evening the proposed meeting took place, and Mr. Wolcott according to my request attended. The information, which had been received to that time, from *Clingman, Reynolds* and his wife was communicated to me and the notes were I think again exhibited.

I stated in explanation, the circumstances of my affair with Mrs. Reynolds and the consequences of it and in confirmation produced the documents (No. I. b, to XXII) One or more of the gentlemen (Mr. Wolcott's certificate No. XXIV, mentions one, Mr. Venable, but I think the same may be said of Mr. Muhlenberg) was struck with so much conviction, before I had gotten through the communication that they delicately urged me to discontinue it as unnecessary. I insisted upon going through the whole and did so. The result was a full and unequivocal acknowlegement on the part of the three gentlemen of perfect satisfaction with the explanation and expressions of regret at the trouble and embarrassment which had been occasioned to me. Mr. Muhlenberg and Mr. Venable, in particular manifested a degree of sensibility on the occasion. Mr. Monroe was more cold but intirely explicit.

One of the gentlemen, I think, expressed a hope that I also was satisfied with their conduct in conducting the inquiry. I answered, that they knew I had been hurt at the opening of the affair—that this excepted, I was satisfied with their conduct and considered myself as having been treated with candor or with fairness and liberality, I do not now pretend to recollect the exact terms. I took the next morning a memorandum of the substance of what was said to me, which will be seen by a copy of it transmitted in a letter to each of the gentlemen No. XXV.

I deny absolutely, as alleged by the editor of the publication in question, that I intreated a suspension of the communication to the President, or that from the beginning to the end of the inquiry, I asked any favour or indulgence whatever, and that I discovered any symptom different from that of a proud consciousness of innocence.[26]

Some days after the explanation I wrote to the three gentlemen the letter No. XXVI already published. That letter evinces the light in which I considered myself as standing in their view.

I received from Mr. Muhlenberg and Mr. Monroe in answer the letters No. XXVII and XXVIII.

Thus the affair remained 'till the pamphlets No. V and VI of the history of the U. States for 1796 appeared; with the exception of some dark whispers which were communicated to me by a friend in Virginia, and to which I replied by a statement of what had passed.[27]

---

26. This is a reference to the following statement by Callender: ". . . When some of the papers which are now to be laid before the world, were submitted to the secretary; when he was informed that they were to be communicated to President Washington, he entreated, in the most anxious tone of deprecation, that this measure might be suspended. Mr. Monroe was one of the three gentlemen who agreed to a delay. They gave their consent to it, on his express promise of a guarded behaviour in future, and because he attached to the suppression of these papers, a mysterious degree of solicitude. . ." (Callender, *History*, 205).

27. On May 6, 1793, Henry Lee wrote to H from Richmond, Virginia: "Was I with you I would talk an hour with doors bolted & windows shut, as my heart is much afflicted by

When I saw No. V though it was evidence of a base infidelity somewhere, yet firmly believing that nothing more than a want of due care was chargeable upon either of the three gentlemen who had made the inquiry, I immediately wrote to each of them a letter of which No. XXV is a copy[28] in full confidence that their answer would put the whole business at rest. I ventured to believe, from the appearances on their part at closing our former interview on the subject, that their answers would have been both cordial and explicit.

I acknowledge that I was astonished when I came to read in the pamphlet No. VI the conclusion of the document No. V, containing the equivocal phrase "*We left him under an impression our suspicions were removed*,"[29] which seemed to imply that this had been a mere piece of management, and that the impression given me had not been reciprocal. The appearance of duplicity incensed me; but resolving to proceed with caution and moderation, I thought the first proper step was to inquire of the gentlemen whether the paper was genuine. A letter was written for this purpose the copy of which I have mislaid.[30]

I afterwards received from Messrs. Muhlenberg and Venable the letters No. XXIX, XXX, and XXXI.[31]

Receiving no answer from Mr. Monroe, and hearing of his arrival at New-York I called upon him.[32] The issue of the interview was that an answer was to be given by him, in conjunction with Mr. Muhlenberg and Mr. Venable on his return to Philadelphia, he thinking that as the agency had been joint it was most proper the answer should be joint, and informing me that Mr. Venable had told him he would wait his return.

I came to Philadelphia accordingly to bring the affair to a close; but on my arrival I found Mr. Venable had left the city for Virginia.

---

some whispers which I have heard." H's letter to Lee, which was dated June 15, 1793, has not been found.

28. H to Monroe, July 5, 1797. H's letters on the same date to Muhlenberg and Venable have not been found.

29. This is a reference to a memorandum by Monroe, Muhlenberg, and Venable, dated December 16, 1792. For the text of the memorandum, see Wolcott to H, July 3, 1797, note 50.

30. H to Monroe, July 8, 1797.

31. H was mistaken, for he skipped the number XXXI in numbering the letters in the appendix to this pamphlet. For this letter, see Venable to H, July 10, 1797.

32. See H to Monroe, July 10, 1797; Monroe to H, July 10, 1797; "David Gelston's Account of an Interview between Alexander Hamilton and James Monroe," July 11, 1797.

Mr. Monroe reached Philadelphia according to his appointment. And the morning following wrote me the note No. XXXII. While this note was on its way to my lodgings I was on my way to his. I had a conversation with him from which we separated with a repetition of the assurance in the note. In the course of the interviews with Mr. Monroe, the *equivoque* in document No. V, (a) and the paper of January 2d, 1793, under his signature were noticed.[33]

I received the day following the letter No. XXXIII, to which I returned the answer No. XXXIV,—accompanied with the letter No. XXXV which was succeeded by the letters No. XXXVI—XXXVII—XXXVIII—XXXIX—XL. In due time the sequel of the correspondence will appear.

Though extremely disagreeable to me, for very obvious reasons, I at length determined in order that no cloud whatever might be left on the affair, to publish the documents which had been communicated to Messrs. Monroe, Muhlenberg and Venable,[34] all which will be seen in the appendix from No. I, (b) to No. XXII, inclusively.

The information from *Clingman* of the 2d January 1793, to which the signature of Mr. Monroe is annexed, seems to require an observation or two in addition to what is contained in my letter to him No. XXXIX.

Clingman first suggests that he had been apprized of my vindication through Mr. Wolcott a day or two after it had been communicated. It did not occur to me to inquire of Mr. Wolcott on this point, and he being now absent from Philadelphia,[35] I cannot do it at this moment. Though I can have no doubt of the friendly intention of Mr. Wolcott, if the suggestion of Clingman in this particular be taken as true; yet from the condition of secrecy which was annexed to my communication, there is the strongest reason to conclude it is not true. If not true, there is besides but one of two solutions, either that he obtained the information from one of the three gentlemen who made the inquiry, which would have been a very dishonourable act in the party, or that he conjectured what my defence was from what he before knew it truly could be. For there is the highest probability, that through Reynolds and his wife, and as an accomplice, he was privy to the whole affair. This last method of

---

33. H did not include any document numbered "V (a)" in the appendix to the pamphlet printed above. Callender, however, printed it as document No. V in his *History*. See Wolcott to H, July 3, 1797, notes 1, 50, and 51.

34. See H to John Fenno, July 6, 17–22, 1797.

35. Wolcott was in Connecticut visiting his father, who was ill.

accounting for his knowledge would be conclusive on the sincerity and genuineness of the defence.

But the turn which *Clingman* gives to the matter must necessarily fall to the ground. It is, that Mrs. Reynolds denied her amorous connection with me, and represented the suggestion of it as a mere contrivance between *her husband* and *myself* to cover me, alleging that there had been a fabrication of letters and receipts to countenance it. The plain answer is, that Mrs. Reynolds' own letters contradict absolutely this artful explanation of hers; if indeed she ever made it, of which *Clingman's* assertion is no evidence whatever. These letters are proved by the affidavit No. XLI, though it will easily be conceived that the proof of them was rendered no easy matter by a lapse of near five years. They shew explicitly the connection with her, the discovery of it by her husband and the pains she took to prolong it when I evidently wished to get rid of it. This cuts up, by the root, the pretence of a contrivance between the husband and myself to fabricate the evidences of it.

The variety of shapes which this woman could assume was endless. In a conversation between her and a gentleman whom I am not at liberty publicly to name,[36] she made a voluntary confession of her belief and even knowledge, that I was innocent of all that had been laid to my charge by *Reynolds* or any other person of her acquaintance, spoke of me in exalted terms of esteem and respect, declared in the most solemn manner her extreme unhappiness lest I should suppose her accessary to the trouble which had been given me on that account, and expressed her fear that the resentment of Mr. Reynolds on *a particular score*, might have urged him to improper lengths of revenge—appearing at the same time extremely agitated and unhappy. With the gentleman who gives this information, I have never been in any relation personal or political that could be supposed to bias him. His name would evince that he is an impartial witness. And though I am not permitted to make a public use of it, I am permitted to refer any gentleman to the perusal of his letter in the hands of William Bingham, Esquire; who is also so obliging as to permit me to deposit with him for similar inspection all the original papers which are contained in the appendix to this narrative. The letter from the gentleman above alluded to has been already shewn to *Mr. Monroe*.

---

36. Probably Richard Folwell. See Edward Jones to H, July 30, 1797.

Let me now, in the last place, recur to some comments, in which the hireling editors of the pamphlets No. V and VI has thought fit to indulge himself.

The first of them is that the *soft* language of one of my notes addressed to a man in the habit of threatening me with disgrace, is incompatible with the idea of innocence.[37] The threats alluded to must be those of being able to hang the Secretary of the Treasury. How does it appear that Reynolds was in such a *habit?* No otherwise than by the declaration of *Reynolds* and *Clingman*. If the assertions of these men are to condemn me, there is an end of the question. There is no need, by elaborate deductions from *parts* of their assertions, to endeavour to establish what their assertions collectively affirm in express terms. If they are worthy of credit I am guilty; if they are not, all wire-drawn inferences from parts of their story are mere artifice and nonsense. But no man, not as debauched as themselves, will believe them, independent of the positive disproof of their story in the written documents.

As to the affair of threats (except those in Reynolds letters respecting the connection with his wife, which it will be perceived were very gentle for the occasion) not the least idea of the sort ever reached me 'till after the imprisonment of Reynolds. Mr. Wolcott's certificate[38] shews my conduct in that case—notwithstanding the powerful motives I may be presumed to have had to desire the liberation of Reynolds, on account of my situation with his wife, I cautioned Mr. Wolcott not to facilitate his liberation, till the affair of the threat was satisfactorily cleared up. The solemn denial of it in Reynold's letter No. XLII was considered by Mr. Wolcott as sufficient. This is a further proof, that though in respect to my situation with his wife, I was somewhat in Reynolds's power. I was not disposed to make any improper concession to the apprehension of his resentment.

As the threats intimated in his letters, the nature of the cause will shew that the soft tone of my note was not only compatible with them, but a natural consequence of them.

But it is observed that the dread of the disclosure of an amorous connection was not a sufficient cause for my humility, and that I had

---

37. In discussing a note which H wrote to Reynolds, Callender wrote: ". . . The gentle tone of the refusal, also, deserves notice. It expressly implies a high degree of previous intimacy" (Callender, *History*, 219).

38. See document No. XXIV in the appendix to this pamphlet.

nothing to lose as to my reputation for chastity concerning which the world had fixed a previous opinion.

I shall not enter into the question what was the previous opinion entertained of me in this particular—nor how well founded, if it was indeed such as it is represented to have been. It is sufficient to say that there is a wide difference between vague rumours and suspicions and the evidence of a positive fact—no man not indelicately unprincipled, with the state of manners in this country, would be willing to have a conjugal infidelity fixed upon him with positive certainty. He would know that it would justly injure him with a considerable and respectable portion of the society—and especially no man, tender of the happiness of an excellent wife could without extreme pain look forward to the affliction which she might endure from the disclosure, especially a *public disclosure*, of the fact. Those best acquainted with the interior of my domestic life will best appreciate the force of such a consideration upon me.

The truth was, that in both relations and especially the last, I dreaded extremely a disclosure—and was willing to make large sacrifices to avoid it. It is true, that from the acquiescence of Reynolds, I had strong ties upon his secrecy, but how could I rely upon any tie upon so base a character. How could I know, but that from moment to moment he might, at the expence of his own disgrace, become the *mercenary* of a party, with whom to blast my character in *any way* is a favorite object!

Strong inferences are attempted to be drawn from the release of *Clingman* and *Reynolds* with the consent of the Treasury, from the want of communicativeness of Reynolds while in prison—from the subsequent disappearance of Reynolds and his wife, and from their not having been produced by me in order to be confronted at the time of the explanation.

As to the first, it was emphatically the transaction of Mr. Wolcott the then Comptroller of the Treasury, and was bottomed upon a very adequate motive—and one as appears from the document No. I, (a) early contemplated in this light by that officer. It was certainly of more consequence to the public to detect and expel from the bosom of the Treasury Department an unfaithful Clerk to prevent future and extensive mischief, than to disgrace and punish two worthless individuals. Besides that a powerful influence foreign to me was exerted to procure indulgence to them—that of Mr. Muhlenberg and Col. Burr[39]—that of Col.

---

39. Aaron Burr. See document No. I (a) in the appendix to this pamphlet.

Wadsworth,[40] which though insidiously placed to my account was to the best of my recollection utterly unknown to me at the time, and according to the confession of Mrs. Reynolds herself, was put in motion by her entreaty. Candid men will derive strong evidence of my innocence and delicacy, from the reflection, that under circumstances so peculiar, the culprits were compelled to give a real and substantial equivalent for the relief which they obtained from a department, *over which I presided*.

The backwardness of Reynolds to enter into detail, while in jail, was an argument of nothing but that conscious of his inability to communicate any particulars which could be supported, he found it more convenient to deal in generals, and to keep up appearances by giving promises for the future.

As to the disappearance of the parties after the liberation, how am I answerable for it? Is it not presumable, that the instance discovered at the Treasury was not the only offence of the kind of which they were guilty? After one detection, is it not very probable that Reynolds fled to avoid detection in other cases? But exclusive of this, it is known and might easily be proved, that Reynolds was considerably in debt! What more natural for him than to fly from his creditors after having been once exposed by confinement for such a crime? Moreover, atrocious as his conduct had been towards me, was it not natural for him to fear that my resentment might be excited at the discovery of it, and that it might have been deemed a sufficient reason for retracting the indulgence, which was shewn by withdrawing the prosecution and for recommending it?

One or all of these considerations will explain the disappearance of Reynolds without imputing it to me as a method of getting rid of a dangerous witness.

That disappearance rendered it impracticable, if it had been desired to bring him forward to be confronted. As to *Clingman* it was not pretended that he knew any thing of what was charged upon me, otherwise than by the notes which he produced, and the information of Reynolds and his wife. As to Mrs. Reynolds, she in fact appears by *Clingman's* last story to have remained, and to have been accessible through him, by the gentlemen who had undertaken the inquiry. If they supposed it necessary to the elucidation of the affair, why did not they bring her forward? There can be no doubt of the sufficiency of

---

40. Jeremiah Wadsworth. See document No. III (a) in the appendix to this pamphlet.

Clingman's influence, for this purpose, when it is understood that Mrs. Reynolds and he afterwards lived together as man and wife.[41] But to what purpose the confronting? What would it have availed the elucidation of truth, if Reynolds and his wife had impudently made allegations which I denied. Relative character and the written documents must still determine These could decide without it, and they were relied upon. But could it be expected, that I should so debase myself as to think it necessary to my vindication to be confronted with a person such as Reynolds? Could I have borne to suffer my veracity to be exposed to the humiliating competition?

For what?—why, it is said, to tear up the last twig of jealousy—but when I knew that I possessed written documents which were decisive, how could I foresee that any twig of jealousy would remain? When the proofs I did produce to the gentlemen were admitted by them to be completely satisfactory, and by some of them to be more than sufficient, how could I dream of the expediency of producing more—how could I imagine that every twig of jealousy was not plucked up?

If after the recent confessions of the gentlemen themselves, it could be useful to fortify the proof of the full conviction, my explanation had wrought, I might appeal to the total silence concerning this charge, when at a subsequent period, in the year 1793, there was such an active legislative persecution of me.[42] It might not even perhaps be difficult to establish, that it came under the eye of Mr. Giles,[43] and that he discarded it as the plain case of a private amour unconnected with any thing that was the proper subject of a public attack.

Thus has my desire to destroy this slander, completely, led me to a more copious and particular examination of it, than I am sure was necessary. The bare perusal of the letters from Reynolds and his wife is sufficient to convince my greatest enemy that there is nothing worse in the affair than an irregular and indelicate amour. For this, I bow to the just censure which it merits. I have paid pretty severely for the folly and can never recollect it without disgust and self condemnation. It might seem affectation to say more.

---

41. See Jones to H, July 30, 1797, note 7.
42. This is a reference to the investigation into H's conduct as Secretary of the Treasury in January–March, 1793. See H's "Report on the Balance of All Unapplied Revenues at the End of the Year 1792 and on All Unapplied Monies Which May Have Been Obtained by the Several Loans Authorized by Law," February 4, 1793.
43. William Branch Giles. See John B. Church to H, July 13, 1797.

To unfold more clearly the malicious intent, by which the present revival of the affair must have been influenced—I shall annex an affidavit of Mr. Webster[44] tending to confirm my declaration of the utter falsehood of the assertion, that a menace of publishing the papers which have been published had arrested the progress of an attempt to hold me up as a candidate for the office of President. Does this editor imagine that he will escape the just odium which awaits him by the miserable subterfuge of saying that he had the information from a respectable citizen of New-York? Till he names the author the inevitable inference must be that he has fabricated the tale.

ALEXANDER HAMILTON.
Philadelphia, July, 1797.

---

44. See H to John Fenno, July 6, 1797.

A Note About the Author

Alexander Hamilton (1755–1804) was an American statesman, legal scholar, military leader, lawyer, and economist. After serving as a senior aide to General George Washington during the American Revolutionary War, Hamilton practiced law and founded the Bank of New York. As the need to replace the confederal government became apparent, Hamilton advocated for a Constitutional Convention to be held in Philadelphia. Following the convention, Hamilton wrote 51 of the 85 *Federalist Papers*, essays and articles intended to promote the ratification of the new Constitution. He then served as head of the Treasury Department under President Washington, later campaigning for Thomas Jefferson's presidential nomination. In 1804, following a dispute, Hamilton was killed in a duel by politician and lawyer Aaron Burr.

A Note from the Publisher

Spanning many genres, from non-fiction essays to literature classics to children's books and lyric poetry, Mint Edition books showcase the master works of our time in a modern new package. The text is freshly typeset, is clean and easy to read, and features a new note about the author in each volume. Many books also include exclusive new introductory material. Every book boasts a striking new cover, which makes it as appropriate for collecting as it is for gift giving. Mint Edition books are only printed when a reader orders them, so natural resources are not wasted. We're proud that our books are never manufactured in excess and exist only in the exact quantity they need to be read and enjoyed.

www.ingramcontent.com/pod-product-compliance
Lightning Source LLC
Chambersburg PA
CBHW020446030426
42337CB00014B/1428

bookfinity™

Discover more of your favorite classics with Bookfinity™.

- Track your reading with custom book lists.
- Get great book recommendations for your personalized Reader Type.
- Add reviews for your favorite books.
- AND MUCH MORE!

Visit **bookfinity.com** and take the fun Reader Type quiz to get started.

Enjoy our classic and modern companion pairings!

Classic & Modern